Fast Cars

Published by Top That! Publishing plc
Tide Mill Way, Woodbridge, Suffolk, IP12 1AP, UK
www.topthatpublishing.com
Copyright © 2013 Top That! Publishing plc
All rights reserved.
0 2 4 6 8 9 7 5 3 1
Printed and bound in China

Welcome to Fast Cars!

If you like sporty cars with monstrous engines, thunderous acceleration and spectacular design, then Fast Cars is just for you! From classic Ferraris to modern Aston Martins, this book will take you on a journey through some of history's most powerful and stylish cars.

A Formula One racing car.

Get Into Gear!

Are you obsessed by speed? Does the sound of a roaring engine fill you with joy? Then read on! Fast Cars is bursting with facts about powerful supercars, classic cars and the world's finest car manufacturers. Check out the photos, marvel at the history and gasp at the facts, as you read through the book. Then turn to the back for a selection of awesome car stickers.

Techno-Whizz

From the first car race in 1894 to the amazing cars used in Formula One today, car technology has advanced faster than almost anything else in the world! Every year engineers are pushing the limits of their expertise and knowledge to produce faster, cleaner and safer cars.

The Porsche Carrera GT costs over £250,000!

Spotter's Quiz!

Once you've read about the fast cars in the book, try to spot them next time you are out and about. Do you think you can tell the difference between a Ferrari and a Lamborghini? Perhaps you could create a scrapbook to log all of the cars you spot? Or why not organise a quiz with your friends and family to test their knowledge of the world's fastest cars? Pay close attention to the car designs in this book. Try to design a few cars of your own. Maybe one day you will design a world-famous supercar of your own.

In Your Fast Cars Book:

- Ferrari, Aston Martin, Lamborghini, Lotus, Jaguar and Porsche!
- History of supercars and racing!
- Amazing supercar stickers!

History of Racing

The first car race took place in Paris in 1894. Since then motor racing has become one of the most popular sports in the world. Every year millions of people watch motor sports such as Formula One and the Indy Car Series. What do you think of these popular cars from the past one hundred years?

Ford Model T

The Ford Model T was the world's first affordable car. Produced between 1908 and 1927, Ford used an assembly line to produce it. In an assembly line, a car is put together by teams of workers as it is carried along a moving belt.

Austin 12 Tourer

The Austin 12 Tourer was made between 1921 and 1939. It was available in three body styles: the two seater, the four seater and the coupé. A coupé is a car with a fixed roof, two doors and a sloping back.

The Austin 12 Tourer is a design classic.

Austin 7

The Austin 7 was so popular that it wiped out most other British small car producers in the 1920s. During its production between 1922 and 1939, around 290,000 Austin 7s were sold.

Historic Racing

A type of racing becoming increasingly popular is 'historic racing', where cars only from a certain era are allowed to compete. This awesome sport is very popular among classic car enthusiasts.

Two seater sports cars have always been very popular.

Jaguar XK140

The Jaguar XK140 was produced between 1954 and 1957. It was called the XK140 because it could do a top speed of 225 km/h (140 mph). Its engine could produce 190 brake horsepower (bhp), which was very powerful for the time.

Old vs Modern Car

Modern cars can be safer, more comfortable and faster than classic cars, but some people still insist that no modern car can beat the thrill provided by a classic. Across the world, millions of people choose to drive classic rather than modern cars. Look at these two cars from different eras. Which one do you prefer?

The Ford Model A was the successor to the hugely popular Ford Model T.

1927 – Ford Model A

The Ford Model A was first produced in 1927 and cost between £150 and £300. It had a 40 bhp engine and a top speed of 104 km/h (65 mph). When its production ended in 1932, nearly five million Model A cars had been made!

TOP FACTS

Model: Ford Model A

Class: passenger car

Style: 2-seater sports or 4-seater sedan

Engine: 3.3 litre

Top Speed: 104 km/h (65 mph)

Price: £150 - £300

The Audi R8 is inspired by the Lamborghini Gallardo.

2007 – Audi R8

Released in 2007, the breathtaking Audi R8 is one of the most powerful and advanced sports cars in the world. It features a light aluminium body available in eight colours, gear panels mounted on the steering wheel, a rear-view camera to help with parking, and four-wheel drive. It has been specially designed to produce lots of power, superb road handling, outstanding control and excellent comfort.

TOP FACTS

Model: Audi R8

Class: sports car

Style: coupé

Engine: 4.2 litre V8 or 6 litre V12

0-97 km/h (0-60 mph): 4 seconds

Top Speed: 299 km/h (186 mph)

Price: £75,000 - £90,000

Technology

Modern cars, especially sports and supercars, are now more powerful than ever!

Engine

The engine in a fuel driven car is called an internal combustion engine. In an internal combustion engine, fuel is burned to produce energy. This energy is then used to power the engine.

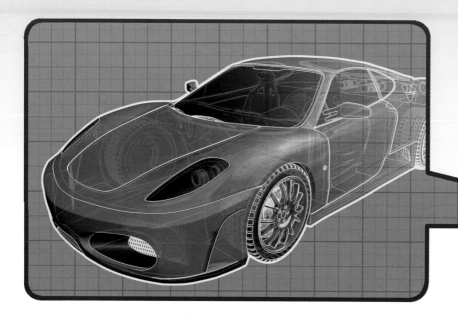

Computer-Aided Design

Cars today are designed using computers that provide designers with 2D and 3D models of what a car will look like when built. The software used to do this is called Computer-Aided Design (CAD) software. Car designers can provide manufacturers with CAD software, which is then used to programme the machines that build the car.

Aerodynamic

Cars are designed to be aerodynamic. This means that cars are shaped to move through the air quickly. For many racing cars, it is important to produce downward forces that improve the car's grip of the road.

Engines can go under a car's bonnet or in the boot, depending on the engine size and the design of the body.

Braking

Air brakes are used on modern supercars, as they are a very powerful and effective way of stopping a fast car quickly and safely. It is estimated that a car travelling at 400 km/h (248 mph), when the air brakes are applied fully, will come to a complete standstill in less than 10 seconds!

Wheels

Most modern cars have alloy wheels, which are lightweight and so improve the handling and speed of the car.

Ferrari

Enzo Ferrari, Ferrari's founder, was born in 1898. The first Ferrari was the 125 S, which was launched in 1947. Ferrari has gone from strength to strength since then.

Enzo

Developed using Formula One technology, the Enzo was launched in 2003 to celebrate Ferrari's first Formula One win of the new millennium. It has an amazingly powerful V12 engine and lights on the steering wheel that tell the driver when to change gears. The Enzo can accelerate to 160 km/h (100 mph) in 6.6 seconds!

Expensive Car

Only four hundred Enzos have ever been made, with the 400th being auctioned to raise money for charity. It was sold for over £500,000, which is twice its usual price!

250 GTO

Considered one of the greatest sports cars of all time, the 250 GTO supercar was made in the 1960s.

The Enzo is well known for its amazing doors.

The 599 GTB is available with F1 gears!

599 GTB Fiorano

Debuted at the Geneva Motor Show in 2006, the 599 GTB Fiorano was Ferrari's grand tourer model. A grand tourer is a high-performance car designed for long distance driving.

Test Circuit
The name 'Fiorano' is taken from the Fiorano Circuit, Ferrari's test circuit in Italy. It is said to represent the history, legend and excellence of Ferrari cars.

TOP FACTS

Model: Ferrari 599 GTB Fiorano

Class: grand tourer

Style: 2-seater

Engine: 6 Litre V12

0-97 km/h (0-60 mph): 3.7 seconds

Top Speed: 328 km/h (204 mph)

Price: £170,000 - £190,000

Porsche

In 1931, Porsche was founded in Germany by Professor Ferdinand Porsche. The company's first job was to build a car for the people, a 'Volkswagen', which was ordered by the German government. The first car to bear the name of 'Porsche' was the Porsche 64, which was developed in 1939.

911 GT3

The Porsche 911 GT3 was first introduced in 1999. It was designed to be an even more sporty and lighter version of the popular 911. The 911 is world renowned for its design and has won many awards since its introduction in 1963. Porsche's official statistics show the GT3 can reach 0-97 km/h (0-60 mph) in 4.1 seconds

356 Speedster

Produced between 1948 and 1965, the Porsche 356 is light and easy to drive. It has two doors and was available as a hardtop or as a convertible. Convertible cars have a folding or removable roof.

It is thought that around half the 356s ever made are still around today!

Side air vents help the Carrera's powerful V10 engine stay cool.

Carrera GT

Introduced in 2004, the Porsche Carrera GT has a rear spoiler that automatically rises up when the car reaches a speed of 110 km/h (70 mph). The spoiler helps to ensure that the car remains stable at a high speed. Only 1,270 of these cars have ever been made. This means that they are very hard to spot on the road.

State-of-the-Art
The Carrera GT is fitted with state-of-the-art technology, including ceramic brake pads, side air vents to help cool its engine and traction control to improve the car's handling.

TOP FACTS

Model: Porsche Carrera GT

Style: roadster

Engine: 5.7 Litre V10

0-97 km/h (0-60 mph):
3.9 seconds

Transmission:
6 speed manual

Top Speed: 328 km/h (204 mph)

Price: £320,000 - £390,000

Did You Know?
The Carrera GT comes in five colours as standard!

Aston Martin

Aston Martin is a British manufacturer of luxury performance cars. The company was founded in 1913 and their headquarters is in Warwickshire in England. Aston Martins are one of the most famous British cars in the world, appearing in films and on TV for decades.

The V8 Vantage has a top speed of 280 km/h (174 mph).

DB4 GT Zagato

The DB4 GT Zagato was introduced in 1960 as a faster version of the DB4 GT. Only twenty were built and it could accelerate from 0-97 km/h (0-60 mph) in 6.1 seconds with a top speed of 245 km/h (152 mph).

V8 Vantage

Released in 2005, the V8 Vantage is one of the world's most beautiful sports cars. The car sits low to the road and has an elegant long, low bonnet. Like all Aston Martins, the V8 Vantage is built by hand to improve quality and styling.

Sportshift
The V8 Vantage is available with a system called 'Sportshift', where the gearstick is replaced by buttons and panels mounted on the steering wheel. Sportshift allows the driver to change gear more quickly.

Although the DBS is classed as a tourer, it is most definitely a supercar!

TOP FACTS

Model: Aston Martin DBS

Class: grand tourer

Style: 2-door coupé

Engine: 6 Litre V12

0-97 km/h (0-60 mph): 4.3 seconds

Top Speed: 305 km/h (190 mph)

Price: £150,000 - £170,000

DBS

The DBS has sleek, flowing curves that are designed to improve speed and acceleration. As well as offering excellent driving performance, the DBS is very comfortable inside. The sporty seats are made with soft leather and bear the DBS logo.

Bond Car
The DBS was featured in the James Bond film Casino Royale. During the film, the car broke the world record for the most barrel rolls. It completed a total of seven full rolls!

Lamborghini

The Countach boasts a very distinctive design.

The first Lamborghini was reportedly made when Ferrucio Lamborghini went to the Ferrari factory to complain about the Ferrari he had bought. Enzo Ferrari sent Ferrucio away without helping him, and Ferrucio fixed the problem himself. After this, Ferrucio decided to start making his own sports cars.

Countach – 1970's

Brutally fast, aggressive and beautiful, the Countach is one of the greatest supercars ever made. Launched in 1971, its dramatic design and swinging 'scissor' doors took the world by storm. The driver's cabin is pushed forward slightly to allow space for a large engine at the back of the car. Most Lamborghini car names come from bulls or bullfighting, but the Countach is different. The word 'countach' is something that the Piedmontese people of Italy say when they see something beautiful.

Murcielago

Introduced in 2002, the Murcielago has an amazing 6.5 litre V12 engine. It is one of the more expensive sports cars, costing around £155,000. Its name means 'bat' in Spanish. The Murcielago is said to have been named after a famous bull who survived a gruelling bull fight in 1879 because it was so passionate and spirited.

The Gallardo is smaller than the more powerfull Murcielago.

TOP FACTS

Model: Lamborghini Gallardo

Class: sports car

Style: 2-door coupé

Engine: 5 Litre V10

0-97 km/h (0-60 mph): 3.8 seconds

Top Speed: 325 km/h (202 mph)

Price: £100,000 - £140,000

Gallardo

Although the Gallardo is smaller than other Lamborghinis, it is a very fast and powerful car. It is comfortable, stylish and even has room for luggage in a small front trunk. The Gallardo was the first car to be released by Lamborghini after it was taken over by the German car company, Audi. Lamborghini gave several Gallardos to the Italian police to aid their fight against crime!

Jaguar

Founded as the Swallow Sidecar Company in 1922, Jaguar is a British luxury car manufacturer. In 1945 the company changed its name to the now famous Jaguar Cars Ltd. Today Jaguar cars are designed and made in Coventry, Warwickshire and Birmingham.

The distinctive E-type design is popular with classic car lovers.

XJ220

Made to rival Ferrari and Lamborghini, the XJ220 is Jaguar's fastest and most expensive sports car. Produced between 1992 and 1994, it held the record for the fastest road car (350 km/h, 217 mph) until the arrival of the McLaren F1 in 1994.

E-type

The Jaguar E-type is Jaguar's most iconic car. Made between 1961 and 1974, it was amazingly popular with 70,000 reportedly being sold.

Most Beautiful?

When the E-type was released, Enzo Ferrari called it 'the most beautiful car ever made'. With its sleek long nose and flowing edges, it has become a true classic car. The E-type was developed from the legendary Le Mans winning D-type racer.

The latest XKRs have the new style of Jaguar logo on the front.

TOP FACTS

Model: Jaguar XKR

Class: grand tourer

Style: 2-door coupé

Engine: 4.2 Litre V8

0-97 km/h (0-60 mph): 4.9 seconds

Top Speed: limited to 240 km/h (149 mph)

Price: £65,000 - £75,000

XKR

One of Jaguar's most popular cars, the Jaguar XKR, was first made in 1997. It is a stunning supercharged version of an earlier model called the XK. Jaguar limit the top speed of the XK series to 240 km/h (149 mph).

Powerful

The Jaguar XKR has a ferocious engine and superb handling. It accelerates with relentless force and thunderous noise. The XKR also has spectacular alloy wheels, ensuring it has an awesome look to match its powerful performance.

Lotus

Lotus is a British sports and racing car manufacturer. Founded in 1952, the company became very famous competing in Formula One between 1958 and 1994. In 1996 Lotus was bought by a Malaysian Car company called Proton.

The Esprit was released in 1976.

A 1972 Lotus Elan.

Elan

The Lotus Elan was first produced between 1962 and 1975. It was designed to be light and quick through sharp corners and bends. In 1989, Lotus released a new version of the Elan, called the M100. It offers unbelievable handling and superb performance at a low price.

Esprit

The Lotus Esprit featured in the James Bond film The Spy Who Loved Me in 1977, where it was seen driving off a pier into the sea before transforming into a submarine!

Tradition

As a two-door coupé sports car, the Esprit has faced much competition from other leading car manufacturers. Its excellent handling, monstrous engine and inexpensive price tag meant it was well able to hold its own! Its supercar looks and powerful performance has made it a firm favourite of Lotus fans across the world.